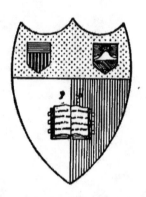

BILL SEWALL'S
STORY OF *T. R.*

THEODORE ROOSEVELT IN 1883

BILL SEWALL'S STORY OF *T. R.*

By

WILLIAM WINGATE SEWALL

With an Introduction by
HERMANN HAGEDORN

Illustrated

*"When you get among the rough,
poor, honest, hard-working people
they are almost all, both men and
women, believers in Roosevelt."*

W. W. Sewall

Harper & Brothers Publishers
New York and London

ET

ILLUSTRATIONS

INTRODUCTION

Of all explorers in strange and half-discovered countries, the historian is the most eager and indomitable to follow rivers to their sources in the hills. Each "crick" is important to him, and the ultimate spring where it bubbles up from the ground has to him some of the glory of the wide and majestic river whose origin it is.

Historians, seeking one after the other for centuries to come to explore the mysteries of the paradoxical career of Theodore Roosevelt, will have more to say of William Wingate Sewall than his Maine neighbors or even the statesmen, scientists, and men of letters who drew him into their councils, when the time came for choosing a national memorial to a great President, are likely now to realize. For "Bill" Sewall was guide, philosopher and friend to Theodore Roosevelt in that period in his life when a man's character, emerging from the shelter of home traditions and inherited beliefs, is most like wax under the contact of men and events. For, unlike Minerva, Theodore Roosevelt did not spring full-armed from the head of Jove. Like other young men of his age, he had an impressionable mind. The photographs of him taken during his college days reveal possibilities of development strange to those who knew the great man only in his developed maturity. There is a hint of stubborn dogmatism in one photograph, almost incredible to men who knew his later contempt for mere theory and his persistent eagerness in seeking advice; there is, in another photograph of him in cowboy costume, a romantic, dreamy, almost sentimental strain, difficult to associate with the clear-eyed pursuit of the naked fact which characterized Theodore Roosevelt's public career. Besides, he wore side-burns at a time when side-burns were already being looked upon as an effete relic of past ages.

It was a frail, bookish boy with whiskers, dreaming of King Olaf and other long-dead fighting-men, who came to Maine at nineteen and struck up a friendship with the brawny

INTRODUCTION

backwoodsman of thirty-four. To the city
boy the backwoodsman was the living
symbol of all that he had admired most in
the heroes of the past—sea-rover and warrior,
colonist and pioneer—strength of arm and
strength of heart, fearlessness and resource,
self-respect and self-reliance, tenderness,
patriotism, service, and the consciousness of
equality with all men. Theodore Roosevelt
poured out his opinions and aspirations to
him, and, hour on hour, tramping through
the woods or noiselessly speeding over the
waters of Mattawamkeag, they threshed out
with grave seriousness the problems of life
and death and politics and personal conduct.
The boy had an unusual amount of book-
learning; the man had a vast fund of plain
common sense. They admired each other
immensely, and while Roosevelt, footing the
bills of the expeditions, was inevitably boss
and felt free to express his mind as such, on
occasion Sewall was not hesitant in "going
for Theodore bow-legged," when he thought
that the younger man needed an application
of unadorned Maine English.

The friendship, established in Maine and

INTRODUCTION

sealed and strengthened by joys and hardships shared in Dakota, endured unwaveringly through the changing political fortunes of Theodore Roosevelt, to the day of his death. No touch of condescension on the one side, no hint of subserviency on the other, disturbed the calm depths of their friendship. Sewall was an honored guest at the White House, as Roosevelt had once been an honored guest at the pleasant house in Island Falls. They met rarely, at intervals of years, but when they met they met as equals, even though one was a woodsman and guide and the other was President of the United States.

"There is no one who could more clearly give the account of me, when I was a young man and ever since," Theodore Roosevelt wrote Sewall a year before his death in a letter commending to "Friend William" the writer of these introductory lines, "than you. I want you to tell him everything, good, bad and indifferent. Don't spare me the least bit. Give him the very worst side of me you can think of, and the very best side of me that is truthful. I have told Hagedorn that I thought you could possibly

INTRODUCTION

come nearer to putting him 'next me,' as I
was seen by a close friend who worked with
me when I had 'bark on' than any one else
could. Tell him about our snow-shoe trips;
tell him about the ranch. Tell him how we
got Red Finnegan and the two other cattle-
thieves. Tell him everything."

That last injunction of his old friend
"Bill" Sewall has obeyed. He has told
"everything," with a sharpness of detail
and a simplicity and directness of narrative
which reveals, on the one hand, a memory
which many a man half "Bill" Sewall's
years might envy, and, on the other, suggests
that "the old Mennonite," as they still call
him in Dakota, has not read his Bible in
vain. It is an unusual record of an unusual
friendship, which historians of the future
will find fascinating for the light which it
throws not only on Theodore Roosevelt,
but on the picturesque figure of the bearded
woodsman whom he chose to be his guide
and his friend.

HERMANN HAGEDORN.

DICKINSON, NORTH DAKOTA
June 10, 1919

BILL SEWALL'S
STORY OF *T. R.*

BILL SEWALL'S STORY OF *T. R.*

CHAPTER I

HE came to my house accidentally, in the first place; it was an accident, but a very good one for me. Two of his cousins, Emlen Roosevelt and James West Roosevelt, were coming up North from New York with Arthur Cutler and Frederick Weeks, and in the station at Boston they happened to run into an old acquaintance of Cutler's, named Andrews.

Cutler, who was a school-teacher and the leader of the party, being the eldest, was asked where they were going. Cutler said that they were going up to the woods of Maine.

2   I

"All right," said Andrews, "but if you go up there the place for you to go is to Bill Sewall's at Island Falls." You see, I kept an open house for hunters there, just as my father before me.

Cutler and his party decided that they would take that advice. In those days it was quite an undertaking to get to Island Falls. There was no railroad up our way then and they had to come thirty or forty miles by team. But they found me and told me what they wanted, and I went with them. They were there about three weeks. I had the whole party to take care of, not to speak of the camp, and altogether I had a pretty busy time and wasn't able to give them as much attention as I wanted, but they got plenty of trout and went home satisfied.

The next fall they came again and brought a thin, pale youngster with bad eyes and a weak heart. That was Theodore Roosevelt.

They had come by way of Lake Mattawamkeag, and it was about dark when they got there. Cutler took me off to one side. He said: "I want you to take that young fellow, Theodore, I brought down, under your

special care. Be careful of him, see that he
don't take too hard jaunts and does not do
too much. He is not very strong and he has
got a great deal of ambition and grit, and
if you should take such a tramp as you are
in the habit of taking sometimes, and take
him with you, you never would know that
anything ailed him. If you should ask him
if he was having a good time he would tell
you he was having a very good time; and
even if he was tired he would not tell you so.
The first thing you knew he would be down,
because he would go until he fell."

I took him and I found that that was his
disposition right away, but he wasn't such
a weakling as Cutler tried to make out. We
traveled twenty-five miles afoot one day on
that first visit of his, which I maintain was
a good fair walk for any common man. We
hitched well, somehow or other, from the
start. He was different from anybody that
I had ever met; especially, he was fair-
minded. He and I agreed in our ideas of
fair play and right and wrong. Besides, he
was always good-natured and full of fun. I
do not think I ever remember him being

3

"out of sorts." He did not feel well sometimes, but he never would admit it.

I could see not a single thing that wasn't
fine in Theodore, no qualities that I didn't
like. Some folks said that he was headstrong and aggressive, but I never found him
so except when necessary; and I've always
thought being headstrong and aggressive, on
occasion, was a pretty good thing. He
wasn't a bit cocky as far as I could see,
though others thought so. I will say that
he was not remarkably cautious about ex-
pressing his opinion. I found that he was
willing at any time to give every man a fair
hearing, but he insisted even then on making
his own conclusions. He had strong con-
victions and was willing to stand up for
them. He wasn't conservative, but this conservative business is something that I haven't
much patience with; it's timidity. I don't
believe in diplomacy. I believe in talking
things straight. It is about time for that word
diplomacy to be wiped out. I call it hypoc-
risy. Talleyrand was great in diplomacy,
as I read of him, but there could be nothing
more deceitful and hypocritical than he was.

4

Theodore was about eighteen when he first came to Maine. He had an idea that he was going to be a naturalist and used to carry with him a little bottle of arsenic and go around picking up bugs. He didn't shoot any big game, just ducks and partridges. We did a bit of trout-fishing. Theodore was never very fond of that. Somehow he didn't like to sit still so long.

That fall I had engaged another guide, so that the party would be a little better provided for. Wilmot Dow was his name. He was a nephew of mine, a better guide than I was, better hunter, better fisherman, and the best shot of any man in the country. He took care of the rest of the party himself mostly. I was with Theodore all of the time. At the end of the week I told Dow that I had got a different fellow to guide from what I had ever seen before. I had never seen anybody that was like him, and I have held that opinion ever since.

Of course he did not understand the woods, but on every other subject he was posted. The reason that he knew so much about everything, I found, was that wherever he

5

went he got right in with the people. Once
we stayed in a lumber-camp with quite a
large crew of men, some of them older men
than generally worked in the woods; old
woodsmen, they were, who did not know
anything but the woods. I doubt if they
could have written their names, but they
knew the woods, the whole of them, and they
knew all of the hardships connected with
pioneer life. They had gone in up to Ox
Bow on the Aroostook River, and it was a
long ways from the road. The river was
their road, and they had made their way
along it and had managed to live there,
mostly by hunting. Theodore enjoyed them
immensely. He told me after he left the
camp how glad he was that he had met them.
He said that he could read about such things,
but here he had got first-hand accounts of
backwoods life from the men who had lived
it and knew what they were talking about.
Even then he was quick to find the real man
in very simple men He didn't look for a
brilliant man when he found me; he valued
me for what I was worth.

The next fall he was up again. We went

WILMOT DOW
IN 1884

WILLIAM WINGATE SEWALL
IN 1884

THEODORE ROOSEVELT AT TWENTY-ONE
WITH DOW AND SEWALL IN MAINE

up to the Munsungun Lakes at the head of the Aroostook River and into the east branch of the Penobscot, that they called Trout Brook. On the way we had to ford the rough-bottomed Catasacoka stream which comes down from the mountains and is very rapid. We did not want to get our feet wet, so we all took off our shoes and stockings. His feet were pretty tender and the stones hurt him. He crippled himself some way, and in trying to favor his feet he dropped one of his shoes. The rapid current took it into white water and it got in among the stones some way, so that he could not find it. He had a pair of thin Indian moccasins with him that he had taken for slippers, and said that he thought he would wear them, and he did wear them and went up into the mountains. He might just as well have gone in his stocking feet, only the stockings would have worn off and the moccasins did not entirely; but the protection would have been about the same. It must have been pretty tedious going, but he made no complaint about that.

On this trip Theodore and I had a *pirogue*,

7

a sort of dugout. I had to drag it a good deal and Theodore had a great respect for my strength. One morning it was raining and I said that I was sorry. Theodore could not see what difference it made, since we got wet, anyway. But by the end of the day he saw the difference, not being able to see where the treading was good.

Theodore was feeling spry that night and wanted to chop. I told him that he must not. He didn't quite like that.

"Why?" he asked.

"Because if you do use that ax," I told him, "first thing you know you will be cutting yourself. Then I will have to not only pull the dugout, but the dugout and you in it."

He didn't use the ax.

Theodore enjoyed that trip. I have a letter still that I got from Cutler after he got back home. "It takes Theodore two hours to tell the story of the Munsungun Lakes trip," he wrote. "And then, after all, it doesn't seem to have amounted to much, except a good hard time."

Theodore Roosevelt was up again next fall and we took a trip up to Mt. Katahdin. The following spring he graduated from college and shortly afterward he married and went to Europe. I had several letters from him while he was there. One of them I prize especially. He said that he was having a good time and was treated very nicely everywhere, but the more he saw of foreign lands the more thankful he was that he was an American citizen, free-born, where he acknowledged no man his superior, unless it was by merit, and no man his inferior, unless by his demerit.

He also wrote that he met some Englishmen who had climbed the Matterhorn. They talked as though nobody else could climb mountains, he wrote, so he climbed it himself just to show them that Americans can climb, too.

I had a letter from Cutler the next spring saying that Theodore was busy studying law and was getting into politics. He was elected to the New York Legislature shortly after. He was twice re-elected, I believe.

He was still frail in those days, suffering with asthma, and one fall, I think it was in 1883, his family persuaded him to take a trip out to Dakota. I do not know who had told him about the Bad Lands along the Little Missouri River, but it was there that he went, getting off the train at Medora. He ran into some ranchmen named Ferris and after three weeks with them he found he liked the country so much that he bought them out.

CHAPTER II

IT was during Theodore's third term in the Legislature, in February, 1884, that his daughter Alice was born. That very night his mother, who had been an invalid for years, died suddenly, and twelve hours later his wife died. Cutler wrote me about it and I have got his letter still:

Theodore's mother died on Thursday morning at 3 A.M. His wife died the same day at 10 A.M., about twenty-four hours after the birth of his daughter.

Of course, the family are utterly demoralized and Theodore is in a dazed, stunned state. He does not know what he does or says. The funeral of both Mrs. Roosevelts took place this morning. A very sad sight. The legislature has adjourned for three days out of respect for Theodore's loss.

Three weeks later I had a letter from Theodore himself. Here it is:

6 WEST 57TH STREET, NEW YORK.
March 9, 1884.

DEAR WILL,—I was glad to hear from you, and I know you feel for me. It was a grim and evil fate, but

I have never believed it did any good to flinch or yield for any blow, nor does it lighten the blow to cease from working.

I have thought often of you. I hope my Western venture turns out well. If it does, and I feel sure you will do well for yourself by coming out with me, I shall take you and Will Dow out next August. Of course, it depends upon how the cattle have gotten through the winter. The weather has been very hard and I am afraid they have suffered somewhat; if the loss has been very heavy I will have to wait a year longer before going into it on a more extended scale. So, as yet, the plan is doubtful. If you went out, the first year you could not expect to do very well, but after that, I think, from what I know of you, you would have a very good future before you.

Good-by, dear friend, may God bless you and yours.

Yours always,

THEODORE ROOSEVELT.

I went down to New York that spring to see him and to talk things over. He said he would guarantee us a share of anything made in the cattle business, and if anything was lost, he said he would lose it and pay our wages. He asked me what I thought of the proposition. I told him that I thought it was very one-sided, but if he thought he could stand it, I thought we could. Whatever happened, he said, we should not lose by it. That was all the bargain there was and all the bargain we needed from him. We knew that we were just as safe as if we had had a contract.

I went back to Maine and didn't hear any more from him for a while. Then suddenly he wrote to me wanting me to come at once. I wasn't in shape to come at once, so I wrote back and asked him how much time he could give me. He wrote, saying that I might have what was left of that week and all of the next. That was something like ten days to get my affairs fixed up, to settle my wife and little girl, and get everything in shape to go to Dakota. Early in July I got this letter from him.

> 422 MADISON AVE., N. Y.,
> *July 6th.*

I enclose you the check of three thousand, for yourself and Will Dow, to pay off the mortgage, etc., etc.

I have arranged matters in the West, have found a good place for a ranch, and have purchased a hundred head of cattle, for you to start with.

Now a little plain talk, though I think it unnecessary, for I know you too well. If you are afraid of hard work and privation, don't come out west. If you expect to make a fortune in a year or two, don't come west. If you will give up under temporary discouragements, don't come out west. If, on the other hand, you are willing to work hard, especially the first year; if you realize that for a couple of years you cannot expect to make much more than you are now making; if you also know at the end of that time you will be in the receipt of about a thousand dollars for the third year, with an unlimited field ahead of you and a future as bright as you yourself choose to make it, then come.

Now, I take it for granted that you will not hesitate at this time. So fix up your affairs at once, and be ready to start before the end of this week.

Dow and I met Theodore in New York. We all started for Dakota together on July 28th. We reached Chimney Butte Ranch, eight miles south of Medora, which Roosevelt had bought of Sylvane and Joe Ferris and William Merrifield, on the 1st of August.

It struck me that the man who first called that part of the world the "Bad Lands" had hit it about right. He was a man named Boneval, one of Astor's old fur men. As the story was told to me, he had charge of an expedition of trappers who had been furring up in the Northwest and had intended to go down the Big Missouri and get back to the point they had started from. But the Indians were on the war-path and it was dangerous along the Big Missouri. Boneval thought that by leaving the Big Missouri somewhere

422 Madison Av.
New York
July 6 84.

Dear Will,

I enclose you
the check of three
thousand, for yourself and
will Dow, to pay off
the mortgage &c &c.

I have arranged
matters in the west,
have found a good
place for a ranche, and
                    hundred
have purchased a ~~thousand~~
head of cattle, for you
to start with.

Now, a little plain
talk, though I do not
think it necessary, for I

know you too well.

If you are afraid of hard work and privation do not come west. If you expect to make a fortune in a year or two, do not come west. If you will give up under temporary discouragements, do not come west.

If on the other hand you are willing to work hard, especially the first year; if you realize that for a couple of years you can not

expect to make much
more than you are now
making; and if you
also know that at the
end of that time you
will be in the receipt

of about a thousand
dollars for the third
a year, with an
unlimited rise ahead of you and a
future as bright as

you yourself choose to
make it; then come.
. Now I take it for
granted you will not
hesitate at this time. So
fix up your affairs at
once; and be ready to
start before the end of

3

this month. We must be on the ranche by August 1st, as I can not hold it longer. So write me as soon as you receive this letter, telling me the earliest possible day at which you can be ready —and make it as early as possible. I will then write you telling the day and I wish you to meet me in New York. Address you letter to

Theodore Roosevelt
care George C. Lee
Chestnut Hill
Mass

and write at once.
Your friend
Theodore Roosevelt

below the mouth of the Yellowstone they could go on to the Little Missouri and follow that far enough to strike back on the Big Missouri below the Indians.

When they got to the Little Missouri they found that the country was so barren and desolate that there was no game of any kind, and the weather so dry and hot that their wagons came to pieces. Their provisions ran short and they had a very hard, difficult time getting through. For that reason he named the country the "Bad Lands." I don't imagine they could have a better name. It is only a comparatively short time, they say, since it was the bottom of an ocean, as all of the tops of nearly all the high hills have clam-shells and snail-shells on them and the country is cut into deep wash-outs and gulches and the hills are very steep. The country looked as though it had been thrown up by some volcanic power.

I have heard that General Sully, who took an expedition into the region and gave the first regular report of the country, was asked to describe what the "Bad Lands" were like, and he said he "didn't know they were like

anything, unless it was hell with the fire gone
out."

But there were times that I remember when
you wouldn't exactly agree that the fire had
really gone out. I recall one Fourth of July,
especially, when the temperature was 125
degrees in the shade with a strong hot wind
which killed almost every green thing in the
country. Some willows and cottonwoods,
that grew in the most moist places, showed a
sickly green after that day, but the grass was
all killed.

To me it was a strange and interesting
country. Some of the hills had been worn by
the water in such a way that, from a distance,
they looked like the ruins of old castles. In
the fall when the leaves turned it was very
beautiful. The hills there are not very high,
but often very steep, and as there is nothing
higher to compare them with they look higher
than they actually are. From the top of these
hills you looked at a great circle as far as the
eye could reach; the only thing that I could
compare it to would be a great rag rug such
as the women make down in Maine, of all
kinds and colors of rags. It was a country

pleasant to look at and always very interesting. Everything that grows there is dwarfed, except the cottonwoods, which grow to a fair height in places near the river. On the steep, rough hills the red cedar grows, and in the fall, when the leaves turn, the stunted bushes and shrubs make a variety of color. Some of the clay hills which have veins of soft coal, get on fire and in cold weather they steam and smoke like small volcanoes.

The first night we were at Chimney Butte Roosevelt asked me what I thought of the country. I told him that I liked the country well enough, but that I didn't believe that it was much of a cattle country.

"Well," he said, "Bill, you don't know anything about it." He said, "Everybody that's here says that it is." I said that it was a fact that I did not know anything about it. I realized that. But it was the way it looked to me, like not much of a cattle country.

Roosevelt had decided to build a comfortable ranch-house at a bend in the river some thirty-five or forty miles north of Chimney Butte. Dow and I were to build the house, so the day after we arrived we moved up the river, driving the cattle before us. It was all unclaimed land along there, belonging either to the government or to the Northern Pacific Railroad. We were simply squatters, as nearly all of the other men were in those days.

We were busy watching cattle until near the end of August. It was new work to Dow and myself and we liked it. It was interesting. Besides, the wild, desolate grandeur of the country had a kind of charm. Back in some of the ravines where the cedars grew thick you could easily imagine that no one had ever been before; but you were generally wrong when you thought that. Many times I had almost made up my mind that I was where no human being had been before when I would run on a tobacco-tag or a beer-bottle.

We started building the ranch-house in a clump of large cottonwood-trees near the bank of the Little Missouri River. West from the house it was smooth and grassy for about a hundred yards, then there was a belt of cottonwoods which went back for some two hundred yards. They were the largest trees

18

ELKHORN RANCH FROM ACROSS THE LITTLE MISSOURI

THE RANCH-HOUSE

I ever saw in Dakota and it was from them
that we got most of the timber for the house.
Back of them the steep clay hills rose to the
height of two or three hundred feet and looked
like miniature mountains. A little to the
northwest was a hill with coal veins in it
which burned red in the dark. To the east
we looked across the river about two hundred
yards, then across a wide bottom covered
with grass, sage-brush, and some small trees,
to the steep clay hills which rose almost perpendicular from the river bottom. Beyond
that was the Bad Lands for perhaps twenty
miles.

Early in October we began hewing timber
for the house and we were at work getting
material almost all of the time until New-
Year's. I designed the house myself and it
was a sizable place, sixty feet long, thirty
feet wide, and seven feet high, with a flat
roof and a porch where after the day's work
Theodore used to sit in a rocking-chair,
reading poetry.

While we were cutting the timber Theodore
went to the Big Horn Mountains for an elk-
hunt. He wanted me to go with him, but I

disliked to leave Dow alone, knowing, if I went, one man would not be much of a crew to work on the house; so I prevailed on Roosevelt to get a man who was familiar with the country to go with him. I never wanted to go on a hunt so much as that one.

In one of his books he tells about it:

The finest bull with the best head that I got was killed in the midst of very beautiful and grand surroundings. We had been hunting through a great pine wood which ran up to the edge of a broad canyon-like valley bounded by sheer walls of rock. There were fresh tracks of elk about, and we had been advancing upward with even more than our usual caution when, on stepping out into a patch of open ground near the edge of the cliff, we came upon a great bull, beating and thrashing his antlers against a young tree eighty yards off. He stopped and faced us for a second, high, mighty antlers thrown into the air as he held his head aloft. Behind him towered the tall and somber pines, while at his feet the jutting crags overhung the deep chasm below, that stretched off between high walls of barren and snow-streaked rocks, the evergreen clinging to their sides, while along the bottom the rapid torrent gathered in places into black and sullen mountain lakes. As the bull turned to run, I struck him just behind the shoulder; he reeled to the death-blow, but staggered gamely on a few rods into the forest before sinking to the ground with my second bullet through his lungs.

CHAPTER III

WHILE he was away on this hunting-trip we heard that a man who was known as a trouble-maker and who worked on the ranch of a Frenchman named de Mores, a marquis who laid claim to the large piece of country on which our ranch was situated, had threatened to shoot Roosevelt. I told Theodore about it when he came back.

He said, "Is that so?"

Then he saddled his horse and rode straight to where the man lived. Theodore found him in his shack and told him that he had heard that a man had said he wanted to shoot him, and, said Theodore, he wanted to know why.

The man was flabbergasted, I guess, by Roosevelt's directness. He denied that he had ever said anything like it. He had been misquoted, he said.

The affair passed off very pleasantly and Roosevelt and he were good friends after that.

Later in the fall, while Roosevelt was away
on another trip and Dow and I were getting
material for the house, we heard that the
same man who had threatened Roosevelt
was threatening us. Dow happened to over-
hear two men talking about us. They were
not unfriendly to us, but they had evidently
heard the threats. One remarked to the other
there would be dead men around that old
shack where we were, some day.

Of course, Dow told me of this and right
there we decided if there were any dead men
there, it would not be us.

We went on with our work, preparing for
an attack. Our guns were where we could
pick them up in an instant. We were working at the edge of a piece of timber and there
was quite a thicket behind us. We knew that
if anybody came, he would come by the
trail and we intended to make for the timber,
and if he wanted to hunt us there, why, we
would see who was best at the business.

One Sunday morning I was writing home
and Dow had gone out for a walk. Suddenly
I heard a great fusillade; something over
twenty guns were fired as fast as I could

count. Very soon afterward a half-dozen men rode up to the shack. They were cowboys. I knew one of them as the right-hand man of the Marquis de Mores, and decided that they had come down to look us over.

I asked them in a friendly manner to dismount and come in, which they did. As it was getting near noon, I asked them if they wouldn't like to have something to eat. They said they would. I told them the cook was out, but I would do my best. We had a good pot of beans that we had baked in the ground, woods fashion. I dug them out and got what bread we had on hand. We had plenty of hard bread. I made them some coffee and got out all the best things we had in the shack. I had decided to treat them just as nicely as I knew how. Then if they started any trouble I intended to make sure of the leader first thing. I think he had had a little whisky, as he certainly had a very sharp appetite.

I helped him to the beans and he began to praise them. He said he never saw such good baked beans and he didn't know when he had had anything as good as they were. I had plenty of beans and kept urging him to have more. I knew that that was a good way to make a man feel good-natured. After dinner we went out and looked the place over. They thought we had a very nice place, fixed up very nice, and didn't find any fault with anything. The party rode off and I didn't hear any more shooting.

Dow didn't come back until after they had gone. He had heard the shooting and I reported the visit. We decided if there had been any danger it had passed, which proved to be true. However, we carried our guns for a while, just the same. I was always treated very nicely by that man afterward and he seemed very friendly.

He was a man who didn't bear a very good name. He had killed one man that they were sure of and they thought he had killed another.

When Theodore came back we reported to him what had happened. We all concluded that if there were any dead men around the shack they would be men that would die a natural death.

We went right on with the building of the house as soon as the cold weather would let

24

us. I remember the morning that we began to put up the walls the thermometer was sixty-five degrees below zero. This was the coldest weather I have ever experienced. No one suffered much from the heat the next three weeks. The thermometer ranged from thirty to sixty-five below most of the time. When it was too cold to go on with the work, Dow and I went with a wagon over the ice to an Indian village about sixty miles south.

Theodore, who had gone east about Christmas, came out in April to see how things were coming on and to do a little hunting. It was about that time that he received a threatening letter from the Marquis de Mores which nearly resulted in a duel.

The Marquis had some time before become implicated in a bad murder case. Two men, one named Reilly, the other O'Donnell, had a shack on land the Marquis claimed was his cattle range. He had made some talk about driving them off the land. Reilly, who was a frontiersman, an unusually good shot, had said that if this was done by the Marquis he would shoot him.

The Marquis concluded to take no chances. With a number of his men, he concealed himself in the bushes where they had a view of the trail on which O'Donnell and Reilly would come to town. They waited for the two men to come along, and when they appeared they saw that they were accompanied by a Dutchman whose name was Reuter. He was unarmed, and all three were unsuspecting. The Marquis waited until the men were in the right position, and then he and his men opened fire. Reuter's horse was killed, the stock of O'Donnell's rifle was shot off so that he could not use it, and Reilly was mortally wounded. But he was a man of grit and determination. He fired several shots at the smoke before he died. He could not see the men that were concealed in the bushes.

Maunders, the man who had threatened Roosevelt some time before, was one of the Marquis's party. The killing was laid to him simply because he was the best shot of any of the men the Marquis employed. The Marquis, however, took complete responsibility and was subsequently tried for murder. Reuter, who had deposited money with Joe Ferris, was summoned as a witness. He drew his money from Ferris to pay his expenses to go to the trial. The Marquis got the idea that Roosevelt had furnished money for the prosecution, which, of course, wasn't so, and closed his letter by saying that there was always a way to settle such difficulties between gentlemen.

Roosevelt read me the letter and said that he regarded it as a threat that the Marquis would, perhaps, challenge him. If he did, he should accept the challenge, for he would not be bullied. He said that his friends would all be opposed to his fighting a duel, and that he was opposed to dueling himself. But if he was challenged, he should accept. That would give him the choice of weapons. He would choose Winchester rifles, and have the distance arranged at twelve paces. He did not consider himself a very good shot and wanted to be near enough so that he could hit. They would shoot and advance until one or the other was satisfied. He told me that if he was challenged, he wanted me to act as his second.

27

I told him I'd certainly do it, but that I
didn't think he would have to fight; that a
man who would lay in ambush and shoot at
unsuspecting men would not want to fight
such a duel as that.

Roosevelt said in his answer to the Marquis that he had no ill-will toward him, and
had furnished no money for the prosecution;
but as the closing sentence of the Marquis's
letter implied a threat, he felt it a duty to
himself to say that at all times and in all
places he was ready to answer for his actions.
I told him after he read the letter to me that
I thought he would get an apology. He
said that he did not think he would, the man
might ignore the letter, but he did not think
he would apologize.

A few days afterward he came to me with
a letter in his hands which he read to me.

He said, "You were right, Bill." The
Marquis had written, that there was "always
a way to settle misunderstandings between
gentlemen—without trouble." He invited
Theodore to his house to dinner. Theodore
went and once more everything passed off
pleasantly.

28

CHAPTER IV

HE finished the house that spring of 1885 and sometime around the 1st of June Roosevelt went east, and Dow went home to be married and to bring his wife and mine back. They all left at the same time. Rowe, one of the hands, went to the round-up and I was left entirely alone. I had plenty to keep me from being lonesome, though I saw very few people for a month.

Fourth of July came, and as I heard that there was going to be a great celebration in Medora, I decided to go and take in the fun.

There were lots of cowboys there and in the forenoon they had foot races and horse races which were exciting to watch. Everybody was comparatively sober and all seemed to enjoy themselves. But before night there were signs of trouble. Too much bad whisky had begun to show its effects. There were

4

some small disagreements, but nothing serious happened.

About sunset the town had become pretty noisy and hilarious. The cowboys were beginning to bunch in groups, and occasionally they went into the hotel for a drink.

I was in the hotel when a party came in. They all drank and then went out, some of them pretty wild. Then they proceeded up the street a short distance, and a minute later all hands began to shoot. The bullets went whistling by the front door of the hotel, striking the railroad buildings or the embankments.

The hotelkeeper peered out cautiously and said, "It's pretty noisy out there." Then he pulled down his blinds and locked his doors.

I couldn't think of any business that I had outside that evening, so I decided to go to bed. During the night I was awakened a good many times by a fusillade, which sounded a good deal like firing India crackers by the bunch, only a good deal louder. After the shooting there was generally a chorus of yells. As I was in a brick house, perfectly safe, I didn't allow it to disturb me very much.

About daylight the next morning I got up to go home to the ranch. Everything was silent and quiet. The greater part of the crowd had been paralyzed and were lying around like poisoned flies, wherever the paralysis had taken them. The town could have been taken that morning by a very few men. The dead-shot whisky had been worse than the pistol-shooting. Nobody had been hurt by that.

I went home and began to get ready for a trip with some cowboys who were going up farther north, to look for some cattle and horses which they thought had been stolen and taken in that direction. We met at Eaton Ranch, about ten miles north of ours, and the next morning prepared for our journey.

There were six of us; three were natives of Maine, one of Florida, one of Texas, and one of Kentucky, all old, experienced cattlemen except myself and one other. The Texan was the boss. He was a good fellow and understood his business. He was also the cook for the expedition, for he had been a rebel soldier in the Civil War and was used

to camping. We carried our provisions on
pack-horses—flour and baking-powder, bacon,
coffee, and sugar—and each man carried his
own eating utensils, a plate and a dipper,
besides the knife which he generally carried in his pocket. Four of the men, the
regular cowboys, took their horses with them,
seven to the man. Myself and the boy who
went with me each had two riding-horses and
a pack-horse.

The country at that time was at its best.
Acres of wild roses were in bloom, and here
and there were plums, wild morning-glories,
and cactuses, which really made the country,
in places, look beautiful. The second day of
our journey lay in more level and less barren
country as we left the Little Missouri and
struck for the Big Missouri.

Somewhere below the mouth of the Yellowstone we saw a white object ahead, which I
took to be a large stone, although there were no
stones that I had seen on the way. When we
came near, it proved to be a small tent. Two
of our party examined it, and found lying on
the ground inside it what we used to say was

the only kind of good Indian there was—namely, a dead one. He had been taken sick, I guess, and had been left there by his party. The next day, when we reached the Missouri River, we came across a party of Indians. They were Tetons. One of the men in our party could talk their language and they told him that the dead Indian belonged to their party and had died at that place. They didn't tell us why they hadn't thought to bury him.

We proceeded down the Big Missouri River from this point, the cowboys thinking they would find the stolen horses and cattle hereabouts. A little way on we came on a place where there was a white man and an Indian living. As soon as we came in sight the white man disappeared. The boss of our outfit wanted to see him and talk with him to see if he could get any information, but the man was evidently afraid we were vigilantes and kept out of sight. At last the Texan managed to make the Indian understand what he wanted and got him to try and get the white man to come out. After waiting nearly all day he got up courage enough at last to show himself and was much relieved when he found

33

out that we were not after him. Evidently he had a bad conscience that troubled him some.

We followed the Big Missouri down to the mouth of Knife River, then followed the Knife River to its head and struck from there westward back to the Little Missouri. That afternoon we saw a bad-looking shower in the west, and as we were going west we were sure to meet it. Five or six miles in the distance was the high hill called Killdare Mountain, on which there was a growth of trees. The boss thought it was a bad-looking cloud and that it might be a cyclone, and that we had better hurry and get in the shelter of the trees. We all started for the oaks and rode as hard as we could. This was very good fun. We arrived there just in time to get our horses unsaddled. Each man picketed the horse that he was riding and about that time the shower started with fury. It was not a cyclone, but a hailstorm, or a series of hailstorms, which covered a space of a couple of hours, with short intervals between. When the shower was over the ground was covered with hail.

From Killdare Mountain to the Little Missouri, we passed through very rough country. In one place we crossed a creek on a natural bridge of clay. It was probably one hundred feet from the top of the bridge to the bottom of the creek and about twenty-five feet thick, and although it had been made by water it looked as if it had been made by men.

That night we got back to Eaton Ranch. We had been gone eighteen days and the boss estimated we had ridden five hundred miles. I enjoyed this trip very much. It was all new to me and different from anything that I had ever seen or done. I was about as green as a man could be. I told the rest of the party the morning we started that I was entirely new, but if they could find anything for me to do, where they thought I would be of any use, to tell me and show me how. I would do the best I could and would be a good fellow if I wasn't good for anything else. That amused them and they were very nice to me during the whole trip. The boss used to pack my horse for me the first few days, until I got so I could do it myself. I looked around to see what I could do to make myself useful, and I found that it was necessary that we

should be up early in the morning, but that
it was rather hard for the rest of the boys to
wake up at the right time. I had learned to
be an early riser before I left the East and it
was no trouble for me to get up in the morning. The mornings were cloudless and beautiful. They were cool, and we used often to
stop from ten o'clock until about three in the
afternoon, and do our riding long in the evening. I took it upon myself to get up in the
morning and make the fires, get the water
and make the coffee, and call the boss, who
cooked the bread, while I fried the bacon and
boiled the coffee. All the cooking utensils we
had were a tin basin, in which to mix the
bread, and the fry-pan which was used as the
baker. It was necessary to make two batches
of bread for each meal, the fry-pan being a
rather small one. The cook used to hold the
pan on the fire until the first loaf of bread got
so he could take it out, then he would set it
up edgeways before the fire and prop it up
while it finished baking. Meantime he put
the second batch in the fry-pan and cooked
it. The bread was good and light. I don't
think I ever ate any that tasted any better.

36

I had a great appetite and everything tasted delicious.

I found the cowboys to be good companions, the same class of men I was used to being with at home, only they were engaged in a different business. They were pleasant, kind-hearted men who were all right unless they had whisky, and were no worse then than our men of the same class under the same conditions.

CHAPTER V

SHORTLY after I got home to Elkhorn Dow came back to the ranch, bringing his wife and mine and our little daughter. Rowe returned from the round-up, and Roosevelt from New York. We then began to live like white folks.

People roundabout used to say, "no house is big enough to hold two women," but there was never any harsh word spoken at Elkhorn Ranch, and I have an idea that those were the most peaceful years of Roosevelt's life. He spent most of the time with us, going East very little. He loved the desolate country, as we all did, especially in June and the first part of July when the rain that falls thereabouts falls in thunder-showers and the country loses much of its dreary aspect. The clay buttes were always barren except for some few shrubs and stunted sage-brush, but in the spring the narrow valleys and

THE STABLES AND CORRALS AT ELKHORN RANCH

THE " WOMEN-FOLKS "
(Mrs. Sewall is holding her daughter Nancy; beside her is Mrs. Dow. The two
other women were neighbors)

moister places were green. There were many acres of wild roses and wild pomegranates; in places there were berries that people called June berries, though they did not ripen until July. They reminded me of sugar-plums and the women-folks used to make jelly of them.

We were all a very happy family at Elkhorn Ranch those two years that we spent there with Theodore Roosevelt. He worked like the rest of us and occasionally he worked longer than any of the rest of us, for often when we were through with the day's work he would go to his room and write. He wrote several hunting-books during those years, besides the Life of Benton and the Life of Gouverneur Morris. More often, however, he would sit before the fire cold autumn or winter nights and tell stories of his hunting-trips or about history that he had read. He was the best-read man I ever saw or ever heard of, and he seemed to remember everything that he read. His mind was exactly like that fellow that Byron speaks about—I forget where, but I cannot forget that line—

Wax to receive, and marble to retain.

Little Missouri
Dakota,
June 20th
1885

We the undersigned, Theodore Roosevelt, party of the first part, and William Seawall and Wilmot s. Dow, parties of the second part, do agree and contract as follows:—

1) The party of the first part having put on eleven hundred head of cattle, valued at twenty five thousand dollars, ($25,000.oo/oo) on the Elkhorn Ranche, on the Little Missouri River, the parties of the second part do agree to take charge of said cattle for the space of three years, and at the end of this time agree to return

to said party of the first part the equivalent in value of the original herd (twenty five thousand dollars); any increase in value of the herd over said sum of twenty five thousand dollars is to belong two thirds to said party of the first part and one third to said parties of the second part.

. 2). From time to time said parties of the second part shall in the exercise of their best judgment make sales of such cattle as are fit for market, the monies obtained by said sales to belong two thirds to said party of the first part and one third to said parties of the second part; but no sales of cattle shall be made sufficient in amount to reduce the herd below its original value save by the direction in writing of the party of the first part

3). The parties of the second part are to keep accurate accounts of expenditures, losses, the calf crop, &c; said accounts to be always open to the inspection of the party of the first part

4). The parties of the second part are to take good care of the cattle, and also of the ponies, buildings &c belonging to said party of the first part;

Witness.

Signed,
Theodore Roosevelt
(party of the first part)
W. W. Sewall
W. S. Dow.
(parties of the second part)

accounts of expenditures, losses, the calf crop, etc.; said accounts to be always open to the inspection of the party of the first part.

(4) The parties of the second part are to take good care of the cattle, and also of the ponies, buildings, etc., belonging to said party of the first part.

Signed,

THEODORE ROOSEVELT
(party of the first part),

W. W. SEWALL

W. S. DOW
(parties of the second part).

I do not know whether the plain story of the business side of that ranch has ever been told. Theodore invested over $50,000 to stock our claim, in cattle and horses—about one hundred head of the latter—and he lost most of it, but came back physically strong enough to be anything he wanted to be from President of the United States down. He went to Dakota a frail young man suffering from asthma and stomach trouble. When he got back into the world again he was as husky as almost any man I have ever seen who wasn't dependent on his arms for his livelihood. He weighed one hundred and fifty pounds, and was clear bone, muscle, and grit. That was what the ranch did for him physically. What it did for him financially was a different story. I do not believe Theodore Roosevelt ever made a dollar out of his cattle or ever saw again more than a small part of his original investment.

Our whole trouble was that cattle had already begun to fall in price before we started and they continued to fall. The truth about it all is that in that country, with the long, dry summers and the cold winters, no one but a man who was an experienced ranchman and, at the same time, a sharp business man could ever have expected to come out ahead of the game, and Roosevelt did not pretend to be a business man. He never cared about making money and he didn't go to Dakota for the money he expected to make there; he came because he liked the country and he liked the people and he liked the wild, adventurous life. The financial side of the ranch was a side issue with him. He cared more for writing books than he did about business, and I guess he cared even more then about doing something in public life than he cared about either. He went East quite often. The politicians would send for him. He used to com-

THEODORE ROOSEVELT ON HIS FAVORITE HORSE, "MANITOU"
(Photograph by T. W. Ingersoll, used by courtsey of W. T. Dantz)

plain to me that the telegraph station was too near, though it was a good thirty miles away, down at Medora on the Northern Pacific.

Roosevelt led the regular life of a Dakota ranchman except that he did a good deal of reading and writing which ranchmen, as a rule, are not such good hands at. He did all of the regular work of the cowboy and used to attend the round-ups that were held within a hundred or two hundred miles of our ranch. For days on end and all day long he would ride the range after the cattle.

In *Wilderness Hunter* he tells about it better than I can.

Early in June, just after the close of the regular spring round-up, a couple of supply-wagons with a score of riders between them were sent to work some hitherto untouched country between the Little Missouri and the Yellowstone. I was going as the representative of our own and one or two other neighboring hands, but as the round-up had halted near my ranch I determined to spend a day there and then to join the wagons, the appointed meeting-place being a cluster of red scoria buttes some forty miles distant, where there was a spring of good water. Most of my day at the ranch was spent in slumber, for I had been several weeks on the round-up, where nobody ever gets quite enough sleep. . . . The men are in the saddle from dawn until dusk, at the time when the days are longest, and in addition there is the regular night guarding and now and then a furious storm or a stampede, when for twenty-four hours at a stretch the riders only dismount to change horses or snatch a mouthful of food.

I started in the bright sunrise, riding one horse and driving loose before me eight others, one carrying my bedding. They traveled strung out in single file. . . . In mid-afternoon I reached the wagons. . . . Our wagon was to furnish the night guards for the cattle; and each of us had his gentlest horse tied ready to hand. The night guards went on duty two at a time for two-hour watches. By good luck my watch came last. My comrade was a happy-go-lucky young Texan who for some inscrutable reason was known as "Latigo Strap"; he had just come from the South with a big drove of trail cattle. A few minutes before two one of the guards who had gone on duty at midnight rode into camp and wakened us by shaking our shoulders. . . . One of the annoyances of guarding, at least in thick weather, is the occasional difficulty of finding the herd after leaving camp, or in returning to camp after the watch is over; there are few things more exasperating than to be helplessly wandering about in the dark under such circumstances. However, on this occasion there was no such trouble, for it was a brilliant starlit night and the herd had been bedded down by a sugar-loaf butte which made a good landmark.

As we reached the spot we could make out the forms of the cattle lying close together on the level plain; and then the dim figure of a horseman rose vaguely from the darkness and moved by in silence; it was the other of the two midnight guards on his way back to his broken slumber. At once we began to ride slowly round the cattle in opposite directions. We were silent, for the night was clear and the herd quiet.

In wild weather, when the cattle are restless, the cowboys never cease calling and singing as they circle them, for the sounds seem to quiet the beasts. For over an hour we steadily paced the endless round. Then faint streaks of gray appeared in the east. Latigo Strap began to call merrily to the cattle. A coyote came sneaking over the butte and halted to yell and wail. As it grew lighter the cattle became restless, rising and stretching themselves, while we continued to ride around them.

"Then the bronc' began to pitch
And I began to ride;
He bucked me off a cut bank.
Hell! I nearly died!"

sang Latigo from the other side of the herd. A yell from the wagons afar off told that the cook was summoning the sleeping cow-punchers to breakfast . . . all the cattle got on their feet and started feeding.

Roosevelt was afraid of nothing and nobody. I remember a "bad man" he met once in some small town in the Bad Lands. The man had been drinking and he had heard of Roosevelt, the new-comer to the frontier. Theodore was not a big man—he was only of medium height, weighing about a hundred and fifty pounds,

45

and he wore glasses. But grit to the heel! The fellow called him a "four-eyed tenderfoot" and tried to take his measure in abusive language. Theodore paid no attention to all this, and the tough naturally concluded that he was afraid of him. Suddenly, Roosevelt let out and caught him on the butt of the jaw—and he flattened out. This gained him some reputation.

He was a great hand to see and hear all of the funny things, and he enjoyed good jokes and stories even if the joke was on himself. At one time he was out riding and stopped for luncheon at the house of a woman who had a great reputation for making buckskin shirts. She was good deal of a character who was living in a wild bit of country with a man who had shot the man she lived with before. He might have been her husband, for all I know, and might not. Theodore always carried a book with him wherever he went, and was sitting in a corner reading, with his legs stretched out. The woman, who was getting his dinner, stumbled over his feet.

She told him to move that damned foot.

He said that he thought that was a perfectly proper way for a lady to ask a gentleman to move, but that he had never happened to hear it put that way before. However, he said he moved the foot and what was attached to it and waited until he was called to dinner, which proved to be excellent, paid for it, and left as quickly as he could. He did not want to be in that woman's way again.

Roosevelt was very melancholy at times, and, the first year we were in Dakota, very much down in spirits. He told me one day that he felt as if it did not make any difference what became of him—he had nothing to live for, he said. I used to go for him bow-legged when he talked like that, telling him that he ought not to allow himself to feel that way.

"You have your child to live for," I said.

"Her aunt can take care of her a good deal better than I can," he said. "She never would know anything about me, anyway. She would be just as well off without me."

"Well," I said, "you should not allow yourself to feel that way. You won't always feel that way. You will get over this after a while. I have had troubles of this kind—nothing like what you have, nothing so great—but I know how such things are; but time heals them over. You won't always feel as you do now and you won't always be willing to stay here and drive cattle, because when you get to feeling differently you will want to get back among your friends and associates where you can do more and be more benefit to the world than you can here driving cattle." And I said, "If you cannot think of anything else to do you can go home and start a reform. You would make a good reformer. You always want to make things better instead of worse."

He laughed about it; but he never said anything more to me about feeling that he had nothing to live for. Maybe he thought I was not sympathetic.

CHAPTER VI

THAT autumn while Roosevelt was away on a hunting-trip I went on a hunt of my own that was as exciting, in its way, I guess, as anything that he came across on his trip; and it wasn't wild animals I was hunting; it was horses.

It happened that in the spring the cowboys of our outfit had gone to ride one Sunday, and when they came back had turned out on the range the horses they had ridden. They did not take the trouble to put them with the main herd, thinking the horses would find the herd themselves. The main herd, it happened, was on the east side of the river. The four horses were on the west side. Instead of joining the main herd the horses went southwest, which took them between the Little Missouri River and the Yellowstone.

We had several hunts for them during the summer, but were never able to find any

49

trace of them. Just before Thanksgiving we heard that the horses had been seen, and, having a little time, I concluded to make a hunt, taking Rowe with me. Dow remained at home.

Rowe and I went directly to a ranch where, we had heard, they had seen the horses. Some of the men there told us they had seen them some little time before, but that there was another ranch quite near where the horses had been seen more recently. It was near night when we got to this second ranch. We explained our business to the man in charge and asked for a place to stay all night. He said he was glad to have us. That was the fashion at that time. Any ranchman was welcome at the ranch of another ranchman. He had seen the horses two days before, he said, and felt quite sure he could find them. He said he would go with us the next morning, as he had lost a horse and it might be with them.

We got up early next morning and started. I never saw such a morning while I was in Dakota. It was foggy and both grass and bushes were heavily loaded with mist. When we first started we could see but a little, but our guide was used to the country and he knew where to go. We went to the place where he had seen the horses and found their tracks in the soft ground round a spring. It was evident that they had been there quite recently.

The fog had now begun to lift. We divided, all going east toward the head of the valley, but Rowe and our guide taking one side, while I took the other.

After riding a mile or two I saw three horses a long way off. I examined them with my glass and found they were our horses and that they were watching something. A second later I saw that the object they were looking at was the other two men, who were nearer to them than I was. Suddenly the three horses started. After them I went, as fast as I could go. They disappeared over a rise in the land and the two riders disappeared after them.

I was alone and some distance behind and doubted if I would see either the horses or the men again that day, but after riding on for a few miles I came upon the two men

waiting for me. The horses had turned to
the right and the men thought I would miss
the animals if they went on. We turned and
rode on in the direction that the horses were
last seen. Finally we came in sight of the
runaways again. They seemed to be trying
to get to the east into rough country. I had
been rather gaining, and about this time had
got the lead and was trying to head them to
the west where it was smoother and there
was a creek.

By this time the fog had lifted and I could
see perfectly. We began to get into rough
country cut up with deep washouts, the sides
being cut perpendicular through the clay.
The gullies were anywhere from six to thirty
feet deep and anywhere from two to six or
eight feet wide. The wild horses leaped
them. I wondered what my horse was going to do. I found quickly enough that he
wasn't going to let himself be stumped. He
leaped the gullies just like the wild horses.
At first, when I looked down into those
gulches, it looked a little risky, but I decided
that my horse knew his business, so I gave
him his head and didn't try to rein him at all,

as I was afraid I might bother him. We leaped gulch after gulch in safety. At one time we came to a very steep hill, which the wild horses ran down full speed. My horse followed at the same gait. It seemed almost impossible to me for him to keep his feet, as it was not only steep, but full of round stones which the horses had started and which kept rolling along with him.

After plunging down this slope, we came to a dry creek. It was quite wide, perhaps fifty yards across. The horses followed an old buffalo trail, which took them down into the creek. From this creek they ran directly into another one. My horse didn't follow the leaders. He took a straight cut across the creek. The wall was perpendicular. He leaped over it. It was somewhere between six and eight feet to the bottom, but he landed right enough and made a charge at the opposite side. I hadn't much time to look, but I couldn't see any way that he could get up over that steep bank and thought he was a fool for trying it. I let him go, however, and don't know yet how he ever made it, but when he finally landed he was on his side and I was astraddle of him on the ground. He jumped up under me. I got my feet into the stirrups and we went on.

We next came to a large and very steep hill as round as a pot. It was too steep to climb and the runaways turned to the right to circle it. I was letting my horse go exactly as he pleased. He turned to the left. We raced around the hill, which butted against another creek. The bank must have been a hundred feet high. Between the bank of the creek and the base of this steep hill that we had been following was a smooth, level place eight or ten feet wide, where the buffaloes had had a trail years before.

Right at the narrowest part of this trail I met the horses. They threw up their heads, stopped, and looked at us for an instant. I thought I could see disappointment in their faces as much as I could in the faces of human beings, as much as to say, "We are beat." They turned and trotted off westward a short distance, then stopped entirely and walked down to a creek and drank. They crossed the creek, and when we got up on some high land I looked back and could see my two companions a long way behind. I waited until they overtook me.

The Texan knew just where he was and what to do. He said there was a band of ten horses somewhere very near and the two bands would fight each other very quickly if we did not look out. There was a corral very near us, he said, and we could drive our horses all into that. We did so, and he, being an expert with a lasso, caught our horses for us.

We celebrated our capture of the horses and Thanksgiving Day at the same time in a way I sha'n't ever forget.

It was two days before Thanksgiving that we caught the horses, and we spent that night at a ranch near by. The next morning we left the horses we had caught at this ranch for the folks there to keep until we came back, and started for the mountains to find the fourth horse that we were after.

We rode forty miles that day and spent the night at Glendive. Next morning we crossed the Yellowstone River by ferry and started for the Kavanaugh Ranch, where we hoped to find the lost horse. It was early in the morning when we started, and the fog on the Yellowstone River was so thick that we missed our way and took the longest way to the place we were aiming at. Along toward noon we began to be hungry. We remembered that it was Thanksgiving Day and somehow that didn't make our appetites any less. It looked to us pretty clear that we had a fair prospect of missing our Thanksgiving dinner.

We began to look around for a ranch where we thought that people might be celebrating, but all of the shacks or buildings we came to were deserted. About noon we got on to some high land and from there, about a mile away, we saw a small house from which smoke was rising. Since there was smoke there we knew there must be fire, and if there was a fire there must be people. Rowe and I began to cheer up.

We rode over to the house, and there in front of it was a man cutting up a pig. Rowe said that it reminded him of the old country, and we both decided that it looked like a good place to stop for dinner. The man seemed to be glad to have us. There were some people coming from another ranch, he said, and they were going to have a Thanksgiving dinner. That suited me exactly right, and as he was having some difficulty cutting up the pig, I offered to help him. When we got through with that pig he asked me to help him with another.

"Bring on your pig," I said.

Just as we got that pig cut up the people began to come. It proved to be Kavanaugh, the very man we were looking for, who had ridden over from his ranch with his sister.

We had our Thanksgiving dinner, all right, and a mighty good one it was.

This was the pleasantest and wildest ride that I ever had. I learned something about horses. A good, well-fed horse, with a man on his back, will outrun any wild horse. I think the horse that has been fed has more endurance and has been exercised and hardened to it. Besides, I have an idea that he gets something of the spirit of the man who rides him. The three wild horses were pretty well tired out. One was a smallish black horse, and at the end of the chase I saw great flakes of white foam fly off from his flanks. I had read of that, but had never seen it before.

CHAPTER VII

WE had many great times together, those years we were out in Dakota, and we had some real adventures like the kind I used to read about when I was a boy. The best of them all happened the last year we were out there. It was this way.

Sometime early that spring Dow and I had crossed the river and hunted for a while in the rough hills to the east, killing four deer which we had hung in a tree to prevent the coyotes from eating them. We knew that Roosevelt was coming out soon and we wanted to be prepared with some meat.

About this time the thaw started to the south on the Little Missouri River and created a flood which, as it worked north down the river, met with more resistance and thicker ice. The flood finally burst through and went down the river with the great ice gorge. As the water burst through the channel of the stream the ice would pile high until the pressure of the water burst a channel through the center, which left the ice piled in abrupt walls on either side. It passed by our place with a tremendous roar and crash.

After Roosevelt came out we decided to go and get the deer. He went with us. We had a small, light boat which we kept for the purpose of crossing the stream when the water was high, as it was impossible to ford it then. It was dangerous enough navigating even with a small skiff, but we crossed and went to the place where the deer were.

Mountain-lions have no respect for deer even if they are hung up, and we discovered that they had eaten our meat-supply. Theodore had his rifle, and we followed the tracks for some distance, but the lions, we found, had gone to some distance, and as darkness was falling we gave up the chase and went home. On the way, Theodore stopped at the shack of an old hunter who lived on the opposite side of the river from us, and made arrangements for the hunter to go out with him next day and camp for several days in

59

the neighborhood and see if they could not get the lions.

That night we had a very strong wind which blew so hard that it fairly shook the timbers of the house. Going out early in the morning, I discovered that our boat was gone. We had taken it out of the water in the only place where we could take it out or put it in, on account of the ice that had piled on the shore. I knew I had hitched the boat the night before, so I didn't see how the water could have carried it away. I examined the rope and found that it had been cut. Near by I found a man's glove at the edge of the water.

I said nothing about this until breakfast-time. Theodore was talking all about his plans for crossing the stream, and I let him talk along, thinking, "Little you know about what's been happening." When he was nearly through I spoke up quietly, telling him I did not think he would get across that day.

He spoke up kind of sharply, wanting to know why.

I told him that we had no boat and explained how the boat had been stolen in the night after the wind went down.

He said we would saddle our horses and follow immediately.

I told him that would be no use. The low ground was overflowed in places so that we could not get within a mile of the stream, and besides that, all that they had to do was to keep on the opposite side of the river to be safe from us.

He said that he wanted to do something and what could we do?

I told him I had some boards, and I would make a boat and we would follow them. Of course, this would take time, but I judged that they would feel perfectly safe and would be in no hurry, as they knew that there was no other boat on the river. Roosevelt sent the team to Medora to get provisions and I worked on the boat as fast as I could. It took me about three days to build that boat. When it was made we took what provisions we thought that we should need, left Rowe in charge of the women-folks, and started off.

It was a strange, wild, desolate country of rough and barren bad lands that we passed through as we drifted with the current. I think there had never been but two parties to go down the stream before in boats, and one came to a sad end not far below where we lived. One of the hunters was killed by a grizzly and the other abandoned the voyage.

We were warned by the old hunter of many dangers from bad water in the stream, but we were used to such navigation from back in Maine and had no great trouble. The cowboys and hunters were mostly bow-legged and past-masters at riding, but they were not web-footed and used to riding logs and handling boats in rough waters the way Dow and I were.

Our progress was very slow and we saw many sights strange and unusual to an Eastern man. One day as we were passing a very steep, high bank, we noticed a great boulder, which looked as if it might fall any minute. We had scarcely got by it when it did fall in. The wave that it created gave our boat a great lift, but it did no damage. At another time we passed for a long distance between very high and steep banks. Up in the bank, perhaps seventy-five feet from the water, on one side was a coal vein, which was on fire, and flames were issuing from various veins on the other bank. I think this continued for half a mile at least, and it gave the whole country a very strange appearance. One could hardly imagine a more desolate region. The bare clay hills, cut up with numerous washouts, and the brown dry grass, made a scene of desolation such as we had never seen before. Game was very scarce and we had to subsist on the provisions we had brought with us. It was several days before we camped at a place where game was plenty. We killed two deer before breakfast next morning, and thought that we were very well supplied then.

About the third day, sometime in the early afternoon, we came to a short turn in the stream where the ice had all left the point. I was steering the boat and Roosevelt and Dow were both in the forward part, talking and having a good time. As we turned the point I saw the boats of the outlaws hitched on the point where the ice had all gone away, so that they could get on the shore. There were a few small cottonwood-bushes from which there arose a little cloud of smoke.

I said to Roosevelt, "There are the boats!"

They had taken off their pistols, and I said: "Get your arms on, boys, and get ready. When the boat strikes the shore you go into the camp as quick as you can get there." I was in the stern of the boat, steering, and as the current was swift it was quite difficult to make the landing.

Dow and Roosevelt buckled on their pistols, grasped their rifles, and sprang to the shore. Roosevelt was ahead, Dow pulling the rope of the boat as far as he could as he ran.

I jumped ashore after him, grabbed the rope, and hitched the boat.

I heard Theodore shout, "Put up your hands!" By the time that I got to the fire everything was quiet.

An old German, named Christopher Wharfinberger, was the only man in the camp. He was not at all dangerous. He was an oldish man; I don't think he was naturally bad, but he drank so much poor whisky that he had lost most of the manhood that he ever possessed. He offered no resistance, and in fact I think he was rather glad to be our prisoner. He told us that the other two members of the thieving party, one a young man named Finnegan and the other a half-breed named Bernstead, had prevailed on him to go with them down to Mandan, telling him what a nice, pleasant time they would have floating down the water and how he could catch a lot of fish, while I really do not think there was a fish in the river for them to catch. The reason they wanted him was because he had a little money and they had none. They got him to buy some provisions, and stole everything that they had themselves.

We searched the old man, took his gun and his knives from him and told him that if he did exactly as he was told we should use him well, but if he disobeyed or tried to signal the other men we would kill him instantly. He believed this and was very humble and submissive. I think that, as simple as he was, he felt safer with us than he did with them, which I think was a fact. I think that if the men felt that it was to their advantage, they would have left him or killed him at any time. We told him to keep the fire burning, just as he had been doing, and he readily promised to do so.

We then held a short council of war to decide just what we were going to do. Theodore thought we had better destroy their camp, take old Chris, and go along. The two younger men being away, he didn't see just how we could get them, although he was very anxious to do so.

As I was the oldest man in the party, the two younger men looked to me for advice. I told them that I thought we could get them. "We will remain concealed in the camp, and when they come back we'll take them," I said. I felt pretty sure they would be back at night. Theodore readily agreed to this proposal.

The river, at the place where we were concealed, had double banks. The water, at the present time, flowed in its natural channel, but at times, when the water had been higher, it had risen above the bank that the camp was situated on and cut a wider channel, leaving a second square bank about five feet high.

My idea was to hide behind that bank and wait the coming of the other two men. They would be obliged to come right up in front of us, as the river was at our backs.

66

Before us, the ground was as level as a house floor and for about one hundred yards had nothing on it but short dead grass. There was no chance for any cover for a man on that. Behind it, to the east, lay a wide stretch of level bottom covered with sage-brush which grew about as high as a man's waist. Beyond that was a fringe of bushes, growing along the foot of the clay cliff, and beyond the bushes were the rough and barren "Bad Lands," cut up by numerous gulches and watercourses.

The wind had all gone down, and it was very still. You could hear nothing but the rush of the river.

About an hour before sunset we heard the men coming, even before they were in sight. They were crawling through the stunted bushes at the foot of the clay hill. They came in sight soon after and started to go up the stream.

Theodore said: "We are going to lose them. They are not coming to camp."

I said: "I think not. I think they are looking for the camp smoke."

Suddenly they saw it and came straight

toward us through the sage-brush. We allowed them to come into the smooth, grassy space and when they were about twenty paces from us, where there was no possible cover for them, we three rose from behind the clay bank.

Theodore commanded them to "hold up."

The half-breed dropped his gun and threw up his hands, but Finnegan, who carried his rifle across his left arm, stood evidently undecided.

Dow snapped out, "Damn you, drop that rifle!"

He seemed to understand that better than he did Theodore's pleasant command. He told Dow afterward that he was looking to see if there was any possible chance and that when Dow spoke to him he realized there wasn't.

We then proceeded to search them. They were well armed with Winchester rifles, Smith & Wesson revolvers, and knives. We took all their weapons away from them and told them just what we told the old man, that if they obeyed orders and made no attempt to escape, we should use them well, otherwise we should shoot them instantly. That was a kind of a fashion in the country and they knew very well what it meant. I then took the old double-barrel, ten-gage Parker shot-gun down.

Dow had cautioned me about handling this gun when they were coming in. He said the right-hand barrel went off very easily and that he had discharged it several times when he hadn't meant to, and, as he knew that I was going to use it to cover the men, he cautioned me to be careful.

I told him I would, but if it happened to go off it would make more difference to them than it would to me. I hadn't come there to be killed, and if anybody was killed, I intended it should be them. I then showed them the cartridges, told them there were sixteen buckshot in each cartridge, and that that was what would follow them if they made any attempt to escape.

I then had them gather the wood for the night, while I watched over them with the old gun. When they had plenty of wood we gave them one side of the fire and told them to be careful and not come on our side or we would shoot. Of course, they were used to guns and had a wholesome dread of a double-barrel shot-gun with sixteen buck-shot in each barrel.

Theodore attempted to talk with Finnegan, but he was grouchy and inclined to be saucy, so we thought the best thing to do with him was to let him alone until he felt better.

I took their shoes away from them that night, and put them on our side of the fire. The cactuses were pretty thick and I knew it wouldn't be pleasant traveling in their stocking feet. After they lay down I took the old gun and watched them until twelve o'clock; then Theodore watched them, with the old gun, until morning. The next night Dow and I took the watch while Theodore slept; so every third night, one of us slept all night; the other two, half a night each.

The next morning after the capture we started down-stream. We did not know that there was an ice jam ahead, but we soon found it out. We learned afterward that that was what had held up the thieves. We were obliged to return to the camp and stay there until the ice started down on the river. It

ROOSEVELT GUARDING FINNEGAN AND COMPANY

DOW AND SEWALL IN THE DUGOUT WITH THE LOOT OF THE THIEVES
(Photograph by Theodore Roosevelt)

was about a week before the ice broke up at all. In the mean time our provisions ran short. We had nothing but flour left, and no baking-powder, and the bread made of the muddy water without baking-powder was not very palatable. The addition to our crew had been hard on the provisions, as the thieves had soon eaten all that they had themselves and we had had to furnish food for the whole party.

This time we were in a very barren and desolate region. Although we hunted some, we failed to find any game. After a few days it began to look as if we had gotten pretty nearly to the end of our provisions of any kind.

We held another council of war. Theodore thought we should have to let the thieves go, we had so little to eat. He didn't want to kill them and he couldn't see what we could do but let them go.

I didn't want to let them go and he really didn't, but he could hardly see what we could do under the circumstances. The ice jam was something we hadn't reckoned on, neither had the thieves. However, I thought we could stand it a little longer on what we had, and perhaps something would happen. It would punish the thieves as badly as us, and, as Theodore was always the last man to quit, he agreed to my proposal.

The next day I crossed the river and spent the day trying to find a ranch. We knew there were some somewhere below us, but we didn't know how far. When I came back at night I saw a bunch of cattle not far from where we were camped. I told my companions of my lack of success and we decided that Dow and Theodore would go down the stream the next day and explore the side we were camped on. If they didn't succeed in finding a ranch we would kill one of the cattle. They took an empty tomato-can, which we happened to have, so that if they had to kill one of the animals, they could leave word saying who did it and why. It was rather risky business to kill other folks's cattle.

They were absent all day, while I stayed at the camp and watched the thieves. About sunset I saw them coming a long way off and could tell that Dow was loaded. They had found a ranch and got flour, baking-powder, bacon, sugar, and coffee. We soon commenced to prepare the meal, as the thieves and I were hungry. Dow and Roosevelt had eaten at the ranch and, of course, their appetites were not quite so sharp. We had a good supper and even the thieves felt quite happy.

Roosevelt had made arrangements with the ranchman for us to get a team there, so the next morning we started afoot to the ranch. We got there about noon and stayed there until the next morning; then we started for another ranch, which was about fifteen miles farther on. The thieves didn't enjoy this walk, but they had to take it, for the ranch was the camp of an old frontiersman who, we had heard, had a team that we needed to take the thieves to the county jail at Dickinson.

We found the teamster a large, powerfully built man with a deeply wrinkled, sunburnt, tough old face that looked about like the instep of an old boot that had lain out in the weather for years; but he was a good man for the job. When we arrived at his camp he stepped up to Finnegan and held out his hand to shake hands with him. As he did so, he said, "Finnegan, you damned thief, what have you been doing now?"

It was evident that he knew the man.

Finnegan told him he had been acting out the fool again. He seemed to be disgusted with himself a good deal of the time. At one time I saw him kick an old tin can and, asking him what he did it for, he told me that he did it because he couldn't kick himself.

Shortly after meeting Finnegan, the old man said to me: "I know that fellow. He was always a damn' thief. I had him in my care once for nine months with a ball and chain hitched to his foot."

Roosevelt took the thieves to town and delivered them to the sheriff, who took them before the magistrate. Theodore made no complaint against old Chris. He told the magistrate that he was that "kind of a person who was not capable of doing either much good or much harm," whereupon old Chris thanked him very fervently. Roosevelt said that that was the first time he ever had a man thank him for calling him a fool.

The other two men were bound over to the

September term of court and had their trial the next fall. They got twenty-five months and were still in jail when we came home. After my return East I received a letter from one of the neighbors in the "Bad Lands," who told me that after Finnegan got out of jail he went up into Montana and went to stealing horses. He was hung there as a horse-thief. I heard then that he was quite a noted thief and rather a careless man with firearms. Just before he stole the boat they had him down to Mandan on account of a shooting-affair. He had got drunk in town and had discharged his rifle. The bullet went through the walls of a building. It happened that the man occupying this building was the editor of a little paper. The bullet passed under the man's chin and, as he had quite long whiskers, cut part of them off. The editor was rather unreasonable and didn't like to have his whiskers trimmed that way. He objected so strongly, in fact, that Finnegan was arrested and taken to Mandan. The magistrate decided that it was only a drunken accident, and, as there was nothing hit but whiskers, concluded to let him go.

CHAPTER VIII

THE morning that Theodore started to Dickinson with the thieves, Dow and I started back to the ranch we had left the day before. We stayed there that night and went back to where we had left the boats the next day. By this time the ice was gone, so we went back to the ranch that night, gave the ranchman one of the boats, took the one that I had made and our own little boat and started down the river.

We then took an inventory of the outfit that the thieves had left. They had entered every ranch on the river, where the owners happened to be away, and helped themselves. They had three sacks full of books, magazines, and papers; they had all kinds of reading. There was everything in those sacks but Bibles. I don't remember seeing any of them. They also had deer heads mounted, sheep heads and everything that they thought they could sell.

We now had a long stretch of river before us and an uninhabited country, with only a ranch here and there. We had gotten rid of the thieves and, although we had lost Theodore and were sorry that he had to go alone, we felt greatly relieved ourselves. We now planned to have some sport. We were beginning to see ducks and wild geese, and hoped that we might see larger game. We had quite a long distance to go on the Little Missouri River before we got into the Big Missouri and had to go through the Grosventre Reservation. While there was a strong current in the stream, the stream was so crooked that we often were going against the wind, which made our progress very slow at times.

One afternoon Dow called my attention to something on the top of a high, grassy hill. It looked, in the distance, like a small spruce-bush, but I knew there was no spruce in that country. He asked me what I thought it was, and I told him I thought it was an Indian with a blanket on. He took the glass

77

and looked and said that that was just what it was.

He said, "What do you suppose the fool is doing there?"

I said, "I suppose he is watching us."

There was a large bend in the river and he was in sight a long while, but we never could see that he moved or changed his position a mite. About the time we were getting past him two wild geese came flying up the stream. Dow, who was the nearest to a dead shot to any man I have ever known, caught up his gun and shot them both down. The next bend we went around we saw quite a party of Indians on the shore. They had heard the shooting and had run down to the shore with their guns.

We didn't want them to think we were afraid of them, so we landed and tried to talk with them. We didn't succeed in talking very much. They made us understand that they wanted us to go to their camp with them, which was back from the river a piece, as it was near night; but we didn't wish to go to an Indian camp and stay all night, as there are always too many uninvited guests there.

78

About the only thing the Indians could say was "Shug." They all wanted sugar. We had a great plenty, so I took a dipper and dipped out a pint, while an old fellow came with his old black hat, which looked as though it might be about as old as the Indian. I dumped the sugar into it. Another one came with what was once a red cotton handkerchief. As it probably never had been washed since it was bought from the trader, I was not really sure what it was. However, I dumped the pint of sugar in it. Dow gave them one of the pigeon-tailed duck he had shot and we went on our way.

After we had gone several miles we went ashore to camp on the opposite side of the river. As the Indians didn't appear to have any boats, we thought they weren't likely to be across. That night, which was quite dark, they had fires on the tops of the high hills. We didn't know what that meant, but we felt sure they were signal-fires.

We had our breakfast early next morning. We saw nothing of the Indians. We saw some white men with whom we tried to talk, but they were evidently afraid of us. When we

started to go toward them to land, they
went in the opposite direction and we made
no further attempt to converse with them.
We were now getting down pretty near the
Big Missouri River. If I remember right, we
got out into it the next day. It is a hundred
and twenty-five miles from the mouth of the
Little Missouri to Mandan. That day we
saw great quantities of geese. At one time
there must have been thousands on a gravel
bar in the middle of the river. The current
was very rapid and as we approached them
great sections would rise. The air seemed to
be full of geese and their wings made a noise
like a great wind.

That night we camped opposite a small
village. The wind was bothering us and we
stopped early and went over to town and
bought some provisions. They told us at
this place that it was eighty miles from there
to Mandan, by the state road. The next
morning we started very early with a swift
current and a high wind.

That morning we came to a place where
there was a short turn and where the river
narrowed so that the current was very strong.

We were making rapid progress and when
we came around the short turn the wind
was blowing straight up-stream. Where the
swift current and the strong wind met it
made the water very rough. We were in
about the middle of the stream and there
was no way to avoid it.

I said to Dow, "That looks pretty saucy."

He said he thought if we laid our boat
about right she would weather it, and she
did. The wave, right where the water and
wind met, stood almost square up and down.
When the boat went into that we took in
water, but we came through. That was the
only place where we found rough water.
After that the course of the river was very
straight. The current was swift and there
was a strong wind blowing down-stream.
We went sometimes almost faster than we
cared to, and the water was so roily that we
could not see anything under the water and
the only way we could judge the depth was
by the swirl of the current. There were a
great many snags, but very few stones and
rocks.

That was the swiftest run that I have ever

had for a long distance. If it was eighty
miles by the state road, it must have been
a good deal more by the river, and we made
Mandan about four o'clock in the afternoon.
There we delivered up the plunder that the
thieves had stolen, also their rifles, pistols, and
knives. We gave the boat that I made to
come down the river to a man with whom we
stopped that night and who hauled our other
boat to the station for us the next morning.
Then we took the train for Medora.

There was a dining-car on the train at noon
and we went in to get our dinner. I suppose
we were about as tough a looking pair as they
ever get in a dining-car. We had been camping along the muddy banks of the Little
Missouri for three weeks and, of course, our
clothes were badly soiled, to say nothing
about the condition of what they covered.
The colored man brought us a bill of fare.
I told him we didn't want the bill of fare, but
something to eat, as we hadn't had anything
for three weeks and wanted him to bring all
he had.

He looked at us a minute and said: "I
know you fellows. I have seen you with Mr.

Roosevelt. I will get you a good dinner."
He did get us a good dinner, the best I have
ever had on a dining-car.

We arrived at Medora that night, and the
next morning put our boat into the Little
Missouri and started for our ranch. Roosevelt
had gotten back several days ahead of us.
When he got back the cattlemen wanted to
know how he made it. He told them what he
had done and they told him he was a damn
fool for bothering so much with those fellows.
They said the thieves would have killed him
if they had got the chance, and wanted to
know why he didn't kill them. No doubt
they would have killed him, too.

Theodore said that he hadn't gone out
there to kill anybody, but all he intended to
do was to defend himself. If there wasn't
anybody else to defend him, he intended to
protect himself.

It was thirty miles from Medora to our
ranch by the trail. We had to cross the
river twenty-two times, which shows that
the river was very crooked. It was probably
nearly sixty miles by the stream. Dow and
I hurried down the stream as fast as possible,

but some places the water had gotten low, as the stream falls as rapidly as it rises, and we had to get out in places in order to get by the sand-bars. It was somewhere near eleven o'clock when we arrived near the ranch. Everybody was asleep, the fires were all out, and we were wet and cold, besides being hungry. It was not long before there was a commotion in the house and something to eat was forthcoming. That good dinner that we had on the train had gotten very lonesome.

This had been a trip that we had all enjoyed. There had been a good deal of hard work connected with it; some parts had been very pleasant and some very unpleasant. It had been a very cold, barren time, for one thing. It was too early for the leaves and grass to be started much, and the weather had been so cold, part of the time, that it had filled the stream with anchor ice. Still, we were all foolish enough to enjoy most of it, after all, and looked back to it with pleasure and satisfaction. It had been quite an anxious time for our wives. The old hunter who lived near us used to go down to inquire for us almost every day, and while he had tried to make it appear that there was nothing unusual about his calls, our wives knew he was worried.

I was glad when I realized that the expedition had come to a successful termination. I was the oldest man in the party, and the two younger men looked to me for advice and were always ready to do as I said, thinking that what I thought was probably best. I felt a good deal of responsibility. The young men were perfectly fearless and not afraid to face anything. They were both of a kind and generous disposition. I had one of the best chances to know the real Theodore Roosevelt on this expedition. As the Indians say, "We ate out of the same dish and slept under the same blanket."

CHAPTER IX

THAT autumn Theodore decided to go on an elk-hunt, and asked me to go with him.

We had been told that elk had been seen on the west side of the divide between the Yellowstone and the Little Missouri River, and Roosevelt decided to go after them. He employed the old hunter, who lived about three miles from us, to go as a guide; a thorough hunter he was, too, who knew more about game and their habits than any man I had ever met. Tompkins was his name.

He told Roosevelt if there were any elk around there he could find them.

Roosevelt told him if he did he would give him fifty dollars.

So we started for the elk land. Tompkins drove the wagon which carried our outfit. We traveled light, but in some places it was

THE RANCH-WAGON, WITH " OLD MAN " TOMPKINS DRIVING AND DOW ON THE WHITE HORSE

all the four horses could do to haul the load, the hills that we climbed were so steep.

We struck from the Little Missouri west toward the Yellowstone. As we began to get to the height of the land, Tompkins protested. "We are going wrong," he said. "If there are any elk in the country they'll be on the Little Missouri side."

But Roosevelt had been told they were on the other side. He said he would go ahead and hunt there first and if we didn't find them there we could come back and try the other side.

We camped that night at a place called Indian Spring, near the top of the divide between the Yellowstone and the Little Missouri River, and the next day hunted on the slope next to the Yellowstone; but though we found old signs of the elk, we came on no fresh ones. The next morning we had a heavy thunder-shower that kept us in our tents until nearly noon. Then the weather cleared off, and the sun came out very bright and beautiful.

Tompkins said it was too late to go to the Yellowstone that day. "Let's hunt back toward the Little Missouri," he said. "If there are any elk in the country that is the place for them." The old fellow knew as soon as he ran his eye over the country where to hunt.

That afternoon we hunted on the slope toward the Little Missouri. Deer were plentiful. Toward night I found a track of a different sort. I was a younger man than Tompkins and perhaps my eyes were sharper. I called the old man and he said it was an elk-track. Of course, it was very fresh, as it had showered heavily in the forenoon.

We went home, and returned to the place early next morning to hunt the elk, but the track went into hard ground and we couldn't follow it. We divided then, Tompkins and Roosevelt going together, and I going by myself.

I found the fresh track of a grizzly that had been made the night before or that morning, and tried to follow it, but that also went into the hard ground and I lost it. While I was hunting for tracks I chanced to run on to a den where the grizzly had been the winter before. I had never seen a grizzly den, but, judging by the quantity of earth dug from the mouth of it, I supposed this must be one.

In that pile of dug-out earth was a fresh elk-track.

I called the hunter and Roosevelt. Tompkins agreed that it was an elk-track and said that the elk was making for the top of the divide.

We rode as he directed, and, sure enough, on the top of the divide we found the track again.

The old man surveyed the country. "The elk has gone over the divide and is heading for the timber," he said. After looking the country over he examined the tracks, which were quite plain here. "He's heading for that bunch of timber," he said, pointing to a patch of woods about a mile ahead. "We'll find him there."

He told Roosevelt to keep to the south and get around on the southeast side of the timber; then he and I would work down from the west and north. The elk would run with the wind, he guessed, and would probably run near Roosevelt.

I went to the north, up on a high point of clay where I could see down into the timber and get a pretty good view. I discovered the elk lying down near the middle of the timber, very near Roosevelt, but he couldn't see him from where he was. Soon after the hunter got his eye on the elk he beckoned Roosevelt to him. Theodore crept forward and fired. The elk jumped up and started off. Roosevelt fired two more shots at him and he fell.

We dressed the elk, fixed it as well as we could, and returned to camp. There we found Dow with a telegram. Roosevelt was wanted at home.

Next morning we went with the team and fetched the elk, and the day following returned to the ranch. We divided the elk with Tompkins and made out to take care of the rest of it ourselves.

Roosevelt was obliged to leave for the East almost immediately, and never had a bite of the meat. I thought he missed a lot. It was the only elk meat I ever ate and I'll say that I never ate better steak.

While Theodore was in the East two boy

ELKHORN RANCH-HOUSE

COWPUNCHERS CONNECTED WITH THE ROOSEVELT OUTFIT

babies were born, one to my wife and one to Mrs. Dow. There was only a week's difference in the ages. We were a hundred and ten miles from the nearest physician. The only help we could get was the wife of an old hunter who lived several miles from us. My wife was terribly sick. The only reason they did not both die was because their time had not come. But both the women lived, and are still alive, and the boys lived to make strong men.

Theodore, when he came back to the ranch, about three days after the babies were born, found me making a cradle large enough to hold both babies. He thought I was making too much noise; thought I ought to be more quiet about my work. I told him the noise would be good for them. He laughed about that and told that story as long as he lived.

That autumn Roosevelt went for a hunt-ing-trip after white goats in the Cœur d'Alêne Mountains in western Idaho. Dow and I, meanwhile, gathered up the cattle that were ready for the market and Dow went to Chicago and sold them. It turned out that we didn't get as much for them as we had paid, to say nothing of the trouble and expense of keeping them.

When Dow got back we figured things over and made up our minds that if Roosevelt was willing, the quicker we all got out of there the less money he would lose. We didn't have any to lose; we were safe enough; but he did. We felt a little diffident about saying anything about it to him, because the trade he had made with us was altogether a one-sided affair; but it looked to me as if we were throwing away his money, and I didn't like it.

So when he got back from the hunt I told him about the cattle and what they had brought. He started figuring and told me he wanted to have a talk with me. I misdoubted what was coming. So I went into his room and he told me that he had figured it out and he told me the conclusion he had arrived at. I told him that Dow and I had figured it up and we had arrived at the same conclusion exactly—the quicker he got out of there the less he would lose.

He never was a man to hesitate about making a decision when he had all of the facts in hand. He was never afraid of facts and of drawing the consequences from them. He said, "How soon can you go?"

I went in to see the women and they said they could not get ready under ten days. I went back in to Roosevelt and told him that we would start ten days from that day.

Theodore left one day ahead of us, and the day before he left he and I went out on the prairie and had a talk. We were very close in those days and he talked over about everything with me. His ideas and mine always seemed to run about the same.

This day he asked me what I thought he had better do—whether he had better go into politics or law. I told him that he would make a good lawyer, but I should advise him to go into politics because such men as he didn't go into politics and they were needed in politics.

I said, "If you do go into politics and live, your chance to be President is good."

He threw back his head and laughed and said: "Bill, you have a good deal more faith in me than I have in myself. That looks a long ways ahead for me."

I said: "It may be a long ways ahead, but it is not so far ahead of you as it has been of men that got there. Of course, you have got a better start. You have health and influential friends. You are not all by yourself. You have a good education and a good head. You have got a better start than a good many have that have got there."

He told me then that he was going home to see about taking a position that had been offered to him. He said it was a job that he didn't want. It would take him into no end of a row, he said, into a row all of the time, and it would not pay because he could make more by writing; but he said he could do a great deal of good in it.

I heard afterward that what he referred to was the nomination for mayor of New York.

The day after I had my talk with him on the prairie he went East, and a day after that Dow and I with our families started back to Maine. Our wives each had a new baby born within a week of each other, called then and ever since, even after they were grown up, the "Bad Lands Babies." We were glad to get back home—gladder, I guess, than about anything that had ever happened to us, and yet we were melancholy, for with all of the hardships and work it was a very happy life we had lived all together. I guess we have all thought all our lives since that it was the happiest time that any of us have known

CHAPTER X

WHEN Dow and I decided to come back home Roosevelt loaned the cattle to Merrifield and the Ferrises from whom he had originally bought Chimney Butte Ranch. They were to have half of the cattle for the raising and he was to have half. The winter after we left was the worst that had ever been known in that region. The snow was two feet deep and the cattle died by thousands and thousands. Fifty per cent. of Roosevelt's herd was lost and I dare say that it was more than fifty per cent. I do not think that he ever got anything out of the cattle. I do not believe the men who took care of them for him ever got anything out of their half. It must have cost all that the cattle were worth to gather up and run them.

I had a letter from Theodore about it next spring. "The loss among the cattle," he wrote, "has been terrible. About the only comfort I have out of it is that you and Wilmot are all right. Sometime I hope to get a chance to come up and see you all; then I shall forget my troubles when we go into the woods for caribou and moose."

He went West shortly after to look at things for himself, and when he came back he wrote me about it. He had just moved into his house at Sagamore Hill and he wrote me from there:

You cannot imagine anything more dreary than the look of the Bad Lands when I went out there. Everything was cropped as bare as a bone. The sagebrush was just fed out by the starving cattle. The snow lay so deep that nobody could get around; it was almost impossible to get a horse a mile.

In almost every coulée there were dead cattle. There were nearly three hundred on Wadsworth bottom. Annie came through all right; Angus died. Only one or two of our horses died; but the O-K lost sixty head. In one of Munro's draws I counted in a single patch of brushwood twenty-three dead cows and calves.

The losses are immense; the only ray of comfort is that I hear the grass is very good this summer. You boys were lucky to get out when you did; if you had waited until spring, I guess it would have been a case of walking.

Please sign the inclosed paper. It is for the witness fee of Finnegan & Co.

BILL SEWALL'S STORY OF *T. R.*

I did not see Roosevelt for many years after that, not for sixteen years—but I kept hearing from him frequently. He used to tell me about his hunting expeditions and how the cattle were getting on. They didn't get on very well, I guess. I have every letter he wrote me.

After the presidential election in 1888 I got this letter from him:

OYSTER BAY,
Nov. 17, 1888.

I am feeling pretty happy over the election just now. I rather enjoy going to call on my various mug-wump friends. I took a friend and went up in the North Rockies, to the Kootenai Lake country, this fall, on a shooting-trip. It was awfully hard work. We went on foot with packs. After a week of it my friend played out completely; he had to go back, with Merrifield, and did not get anything at all. I kept on, with a white man and an Indian; after a while I got some pretty fair hunting; among other things I killed a big black bear and a fine bull caribou. I saw Blaine the other day and had a pleasant talk with him.

A year later he went out West again, and when he got back he wrote me about it:

Oct. 13, 1889.

I went over into the Idaho country and had very good luck; among other things I killed a panther, two bull moose, and two grizzlies; one of the last made a most determined charge, but I stopped him with the old Winchester. I still keep the Elkhorn ranch-house open, but will probably close it for good next year. I am picking up a little in the cattle business, branding a slightly larger number of calves each year, and putting back a few thousand dollars into my capital; but I shall never make good my losses.

He used to write me something of his life in Washington as Civil Service Commissioner, and of the men in Congress from my state; he knew I would be interested. On February 25, 1891, he wrote me from Washington:

I have seen a great deal of Tom Reed this winter, and my liking for him has grown. He is a very strong man, and has done more to help along public business than any Speaker I have ever known. I like Boutelle, too, and Frye and Dingley. I have also seen very much of Blaine. He is certainly a very shrewd and able man and he has been most hospitable to me. All the Maine delegation are pretty bright men, which is more than can be said for New York with its large Tammany Hall contingent.

Wilmot Dow died that spring. Theodore had been mighty fond of him. He wrote me how sorry he was:

I cannot realize that he, so lusty and powerful and healthy, can have gone. You know how highly I esteemed Wilmot. He was one of the men whom I felt proud to have as a friend and he has left his children the name of an upright and honorable man who played his part manfully in the world. His sincerity and strength of character, his courage, his gentleness to his wife, his loyalty to his friends, all made him one whose loss must be greatly mourned by whoever had had the good fortune to be thrown intimately with him; to his wife and children, and to you, his loss is irreparable. May we all do our duty as straightforwardly and well as he did his.

That was in May. In August he wrote again, telling me about the birth of his daughter Ethel. He was still full of thoughts of Will Dow.

I think of Wilmot all the time; I can see him riding a bucker, or paddling a canoe, or shooting an antelope; or doing the washing for his wife, or playing with the children. If ever there was a fine, noble fellow, he was one.

I did not hear from him again for a year after that. But in the fall of 1892 he went West again and he knew I would be interested in how he found things out there, so he wrote me about it:

I spent three weeks out West this year; first at my ranch, and then on a wagon trip down to the Black Hills, during the course of which I shot a few antelope. My cattle are doing a little better than they were. The ranch-house is in good repair, but of course it is melancholy to see it deserted; I stayed there several days. One morning, as I was sitting on the piazza, I heard a splashing in the river (nearly where Bill Rowe drowned Cropears) and there were three deer! They walked up along the sand to the crossing; and I picked up my rifle, leaned against one of the big cottonwoods, and dropped one in its tracks. We were out of meat and the venison tasted first rate. I never expected to shoot a deer from the piazza.

He was having a pretty difficult time on the Civil Service Commission about this time with the people who didn't believe in civil service reform and wanted their friends appointed to office by the old spoils system that Roosevelt was trying to put out of business. Every little while one of the rows he was having would get into the papers. I wrote him once telling him that I was glad he was keeping in fighting trim and I got this letter back from him:

WASHINGTON,
Dec. 28, 1893.

Yes, I *did* have a savage time of it with that unreconstructed rebel. He was a real type of the fire-eater; he always went armed with a revolver and was always bullying and threatening and talking about his deeds as a General in the War, and "his people" the Southerners, and "his party" the Democrats. He was a big fellow, and once or twice I wished I had your thews; but as I had not, I resolved to do what I could with my own if it came to a rough and tumble. However, he was like the Marquis, that time he wrote me the note when we were all at the ranch. After he had carried his bullying to a certain point I brought him up with a round turn, and when he threatened I told him to go right ahead, that I was no brawler, but that I was always ready to defend myself in any way, and that, moreover, I could guarantee to do it, too. Then he backed off. I was always having difficulties with him as he was an inveterate hater of Republicans in general, of Northerners and especially of negroes. However, I finally drove him off the Commission; and before this happened had reduced him to absolute impotence on the Commission, save that he could still be a temporary obstructionist. I am well, though I don't get any exercise now; and this has been a very hard business year.

When the Spanish War came I was one of those who thought he had no business himself to go to war. I never was a pacifist in my life any more than he was. Neither of us wanted to pick a quarrel, but when a quarrel came we weren't the men to dodge it. It seemed to me, however, that it wasn't his place to go to Cuba. I thought he had more important work to do in the Navy Department and I wrote him so. I never expected him to answer my letter. The Navy Department was a pretty busy place at that time. I knew that well enough and I doubted whether my letter would even ever reach him. But his answer came just as quick as the mails could carry it, and was written on April 23, 1898, the very day that Congress declared war. Here is the letter:

NAVY DEPT., WASHINGTON.

I thank you for your advice, old man, but it seems to me that if I can go I better had. My work here has been the work of preparing the tools. They are prepared, and now the work must lie with those who use them. The work of preparation is done; the work of using the tools has begun. If possible I would like to be one of those who use the tools.

Well, he was one of those who used the tools, and pretty soon everybody all over the country knew how well he had used them. I never doubted that he would make a good soldier. He would have made good at pretty nearly anything, except, perhaps, as a money-maker, and he would have made good at that, too, if he had ever cared to put his mind to it.

The first thing I knew I was writing to a man who was Governor of New York. We corresponded quite a good deal those years.

He seemed to be interested in getting my point of view on things, and it happened that we always agreed on the fundamental things, just as we had agreed when we were in Maine and Dakota together. Separation didn't seem to make any difference. I hadn't seen Theodore for twelve years, but our minds seemed to run just like a team.

Two weeks after he was inaugurated as governor he wrote me:

ALBANY,
Jan. 18, 1899.

What you say about the reformers is exactly true. People like to talk about reform, but they don't want to give one hour's work or five cents' worth of time. They would much rather sit at home and grumble at the men who really do do the work, because these men, like all other men, are sure to make mistakes sometimes.

I have had a pretty busy year, but I have enjoyed it all and I am proud of being governor and am going to try and make a square and decent one. I do not expect, however, to hold political office again, and in one way that is a help, because the politicians cannot threaten me with what they will do in the future.

Six months later I heard from him again:

OYSTER BAY,
July 8, 1899.

You are right about the courage needed in a position like this being quite as much if not more than that needed at San Juan Hill. The trouble is that right and wrong so often do not come up sharply divided. If I am sure a thing is either right or wrong, why then I know how to act, but lots of times there is a little of both on each side, and then it becomes mighty puzzling to know the exact course to follow.

In the spring of 1900 I wrote him about the Boer War, saying that my sympathies were rather with the British, and I received this letter:

ALBANY,
April 24, 1900.

As to the Boer War, you have hit my opinion almost exactly. The British behaved so well to us during the Spanish War that I have no patience with these people who keep howling against them. I was mighty glad to see them conquer the Mahdi for the same reason that I think we should conquer Aguinaldo. The Sudan and Matabeleland will be better off under England's rule, just as the Philippines will be under our rule. But as against the Boers, I think the policy of Rhodes and Chamberlain has been one huge blunder, and exactly as you say, the British have won only by crushing superiority in numbers where they have won at all. Generally they have been completely outfought, while some of their blunders have been simply stupendous. Now of course I think it would be a great deal better if all the white people of South Africa spoke English, and if my Dutch kinsfolk over there grew to accept English as their language just as my people and I here have done, they would be a great deal better off. The

9   105

more I have looked into this Boer War the more un-comfortable I have felt about it. Of course, this is for your eyes only. I do not want to mix in things which do not concern me, and I have no patience with the Senators and Representatives that attend anti-British meetings and howl about England. I notice that they are generally men that sympathized with Spain two years ago.

CHAPTER XI

I DID not see Theodore for sixteen years altogether and when I saw him again he was President of the United States.

It was shortly after McKinley was assassinated. He was to come to Bangor to speak. I did not write to him; I made up my mind that I would be there. I suppose he knew that I would be there, just the same as I knew that he would be looking for me. When he came into the state he began to inquire for me. I went to the Bangor House and the Congressman from my district was there and asked me if I was not going down to meet the President's train.

I told him no, there was no use of my going down there. I said, "I want to see Roosevelt. If I go down there, I shall not be able to, there will be so many of you fellows around him." So I told him, "If he inquires for me, you will know where I am; I'm going to be right here."

When he arrived at the hotel they had dinner prepared there and they wanted him to go up before dinner and make a speech from the balcony. He said he would, but when he stepped out on the balcony he said to the crowd that was gathered below that before he started with a speech he wanted to act the part of town-crier; he wanted to know if there was anybody there who knew Bill Sewall and knew whether he was there that day or not. There was somebody in the neighborhood who did know me, a man who boarded with me, and the Congressman told him that he knew where I was.

This man came in to where I was and told me that I had been called for and that I was wanted for dinner.

Theodore finished his speech and then in a little room next to the dining-room he met us alone, my wife and myself and Will Dow's wife, who had married again and was there with her husband, Fleetwood Pride. We talked over the ranch days and it was just as though we were back there again together.

He had to make another speech at a town near by that afternoon and he took me along with him. We had quite a little talk on the way.

I said to him, "Do you remember what I told you when you were in Dakota?"

He said: "Yes. How strange that you knew it!"

I said: "It was not strange to me. I did not expect to see you made President this way." I said: "I did not suppose you would be shot into the Presidency, but I expected to see you President in a different manner, and I expect to yet. We will do that next time."

While he was at Bangor Theodore invited me to come to the White House during the coming winter and bring my family and my two brothers and their families and Mrs. Pride and her husband. I reckoned it up at the time; I think he asked twenty-five of us all in all. He said, "We'll all break bread in the White House."

Less than a week later I had a letter from him thanking my wife and Mrs. Pride for some hunting socks that they had knitted for him and then saying:

Now on Jan'y 22nd we have the Judicial reception and on February 5 the Congressional reception. I would like to have you come down here the day before one of these two days. I think the Congressional reception you would probably enjoy most. If you like, I will have quarters engaged for you either at a particular house or hotel as you tell me to do. Then I will have Franklin Hall, who acts as messenger for me, meet you at the train when you tell me the train you will come by, and take you first to your quarters and then up to the White House; and I shall have him detailed to show you all around the sights here while you are in town. I look forward to seeing all of you.

The letter was typewritten, but under it, in his own hand, he wrote: *"Come sure. We'll have a celebration. Your friend, Theodore Roosevelt."*

My brothers, being very old, could not go, but my wife and myself, with our two older children and Mr. and Mrs. Pride and their son, went.

We went to our boarding-place as he had directed, and then we went to the White House. He was not there when we arrived, for it was in the afternoon and he was out riding. By and by we heard a door open, then we heard his quick step in the hall, and it was for all the world like the way he used

to come down the long hall at Elkhorn
Ranch; and when he came into the room in
his riding-clothes it seemed as though these
sixteen years that lay between had never
been and we were all back in the happy
ranch days again.

He took us all over the White House that
afternoon.

"How do you like it, Bill?" he asked me.

"Why," I said, "it looks to me as how
you've got a pretty good camp."

"It's always a good thing to have a good
camp," he said.

Mrs. Roosevelt kind of took the manage-
ment of us while we were in town and looked
to it that we saw Mount Vernon and all the
other sights. I guess we had as fine a time
as anybody that ever came to Washington,
and when we seemed to attract a good deal
of attention, sitting in the President's box
at the theater, I told the ladies, who were
rather bothered by it, that it was perfectly
natural—the people had found something
green from the country.

I saw him once or twice again during his
Presidency, at the White House and at

Oyster Bay, and every little while out of
the midst of the fight he was in he would
send me a letter telling me something about
it. Here is one of them, written on September
22, 1903:

Sometimes I feel a little melancholy because it is
so hard to persuade people to accept equal justice.
The very rich corporation people are sore and angry
because I refuse to allow a case like that of the Northern
Securities Company to go unchallenged by the law;
and in the same way the turbulent and extreme labor
union people are sore and angry because I insist that
every man, whether he belong to a labor union or not,
shall be given a square deal in government employment.
Now, I believe in rich people who act squarely, and in
labor unions which are managed with wisdom and justice; but when either employee or employer, laboring
man or capitalist, goes wrong, I have to clinch him, and
that is all there is to it.

In the spring of 1906 I wrote him telling
him what a fine job I thought he was doing
in Washington. This was his answer:

June 13, 1906.

I am mighty glad you like what I have been doing
in the governmental field. I do not have to tell you that
my great hero is Abraham Lincoln, and I have wanted
while President to be the representative of the "plain
people" in the same sense that he was—not, of course,

with the genius and power that he had, but, according to my lights, along the same lines.

Just after the Republican Convention in Chicago that nominated Taft in 1908 he wrote me again:

June 25, 1908.

I hope Mrs. Roosevelt will be better now, when the strain of the Presidency is off her. As for me, I have thoroughly enjoyed the job. I never felt more vigorous, so far as the work of the office is concerned, and if I had followed my own desires I should have been only too delighted to stay as President. I had said that I would not accept another term, and I believe the people think that my word is good, and I should be mighty sorry to have them think anything else. However, for the very reason that I believe in being a strong President and making the most of the office and using it without regard to the little, feeble, snarling men who yell about executive usurpation, I also believe that it is not a good thing that any one man should hold it too long. My ambition is, in however humble a manner and however far off, to travel in the footsteps of Washington and Lincoln.

I think he did travel in the footsteps of Washington and Lincoln, and what pleased me most about him was to see him, now that he was in power, put into practice the principles he had expressed when he was a boy in Maine and when he was a young man in

Dakota. It just seemed to me that he was giving public expression to what I had always known was in him. I think I agreed with pretty near everything that he did, and when he came out for the Republican nomination in the spring of 1912 I was with him with all the strength that I possessed.

He remembered those talks that we had together, just as I remembered them. On May 28, 1912, he wrote me:

Your letter contains really the philosophy of my canvass. After all, I am merely standing for the principles which you and I used to discuss so often in the old days both in the Maine woods and along the Little Missouri. They are the principles of real Americans and I believe that more and more the plain people of the country are waking up to the fact that they are the right principles.

CHAPTER XII

HE is dead now and all the world is seeing what I saw forty years ago, and saying about him what I said when we lived under the same roof in the Dakota days. I knew him well, for I saw him under all conditions. He was always the same stanch gentleman, always a defender of right as he saw it, and he saw right himself. It is no use for me to name his good qualities. It is enough for me to say that I think he had more than any man I have ever known and more than any man the world has produced since Lincoln.

I have not read so much as many men, but I have read something about many great men, and I do not think that in nineteen hundred years there has been any man who had so many good qualities and knew how to use them as well as he did. He was a fighter, but in this he only resembled Pe ter Peter was always ready to fight. But Roosevelt was always ready to live by the Golden Rule. If he had been in a position of power in 1914 and if the nations had been ready to follow him, I think we would not have had this war, and a good deal that may yet come. There have been many great men in the history of the world, but they have almost always had some bad defects. Theodore Roosevelt's defects were not great— and such as they were Time will only soften them.

THE END